# Those *Amazing*
# Engineers

WRITTEN BY
**CHARLOTTE FORBES**

DESIGN AND ILLUSTRATION BY
**DEAN PILLION**

**Those Amazing™. Series**

Trilogy Publications LLC
Englewood Cliffs, New Jersey 07632

# Table of Contents

SECOND EDITION, REVISED
Second Edition published 2006
First Edition published 2004

Written by Charlotte Forbes
Design and Illustration by Dean Pillion
Art Direction by Mark Lo Bello
Edited by Rose Reichman and Rena Frankle

ISBN 978-0-9772799-0-6

# Those Amazing Engineers

Have you ever crossed a bridge? Played a video game? Flipped on a light switch? Eaten a jelly bean or listened to an iPod®? Then you've sampled what an engineer does. Engineers touch every part of our lives. Anything that makes our world better, safer and more fun is the work of an engineer. Engineers make a difference!

Most people think of artists and musicians as creative. Engineers are creative, too. In fact, they're some of the most creative people around. There are many, many kinds of engineers. Some engineers design and build the roads that get us where we want to go. Others invent new machines, like robot-building robots, or develop materials to make things like lighter tennis rackets and faster skis. Still others soup up supercomputers, clean our air, put an astronaut in space. And can you believe it? It was an engineer who invented the Slinky®!

If you grow up to be an engineer, you'll do some amazing things!

**Future Engineers**

# Aerospace Engineers
## The Sky's the Limit (*not*)

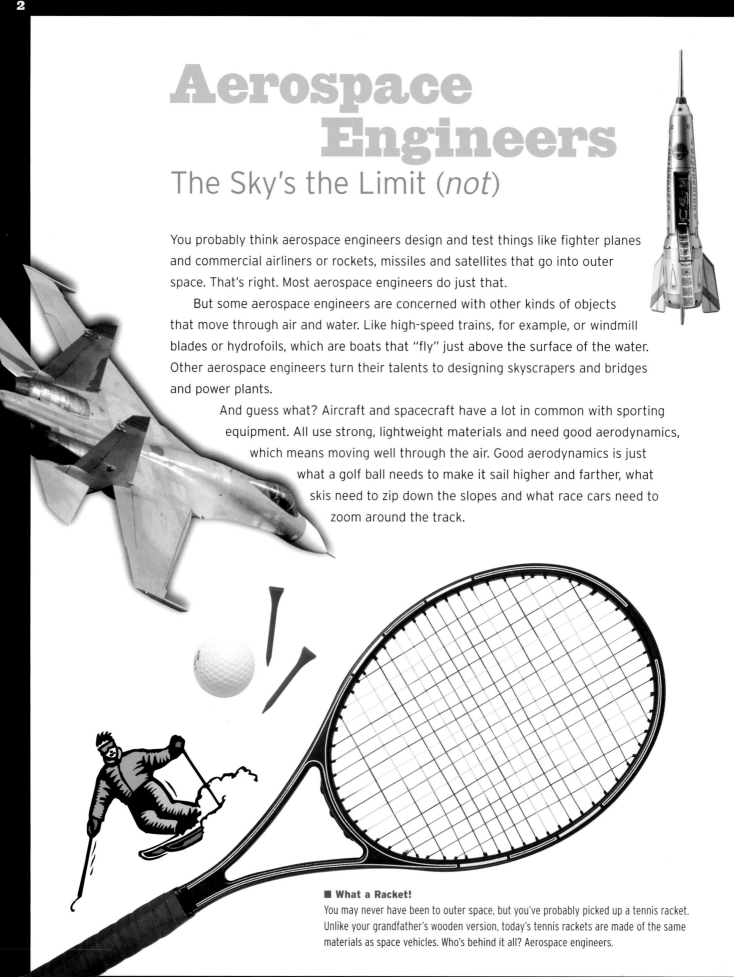

You probably think aerospace engineers design and test things like fighter planes and commercial airliners or rockets, missiles and satellites that go into outer space. That's right. Most aerospace engineers do just that.

But some aerospace engineers are concerned with other kinds of objects that move through air and water. Like high-speed trains, for example, or windmill blades or hydrofoils, which are boats that "fly" just above the surface of the water. Other aerospace engineers turn their talents to designing skyscrapers and bridges and power plants.

And guess what? Aircraft and spacecraft have a lot in common with sporting equipment. All use strong, lightweight materials and need good aerodynamics, which means moving well through the air. Good aerodynamics is just what a golf ball needs to make it sail higher and farther, what skis need to zip down the slopes and what race cars need to zoom around the track.

### ■ What a Racket!
You may never have been to outer space, but you've probably picked up a tennis racket. Unlike your grandfather's wooden version, today's tennis rackets are made of the same materials as space vehicles. Who's behind it all? Aerospace engineers.

**■ Weather Forecast**

So it's going to rain on Wednesday. How do we know? Aerospace engineers design satellites that orbit our planet, measuring things like cloud cover, temperature, moisture and wind speed. With the help of powerful computers, scientists use that information to predict the weather.

**■ A Station in Space**

What weighs more than 1 million pounds, has research labs, is a temporary home for humans and is floating around in space? The International Space Station. It's the largest and most complex international science project in history. Since 2000, crews—including engineers—have been living at the station, doing research in medicine and science that will help everyone. Sometimes, they even take a little walk in space. Chalk one up for aerospace engineers! Try to catch a glimpse of the station some clear night. Check out **www.heavens-above.com** for information on when it's visible from where you live.

**■ On to Pluto**

No, not the cartoon character, the dwarf planet at the edge of our solar system. Aerospace engineers helped launch NASA's New Horizon satellite, which is speeding toward Pluto at 50,000 miles per hour. Look for pictures to arrive back in 2015.

you are here!

Mercury   Venus   Earth   Mars   Jupiter   Saturn   Uranus   Neptune   Pluto

# Chemical Engineers
## Presto-Change-o

Chemical engineers take chemistry out of the lab and into the factory to produce things you depend on. Your toothpaste, for example. And your skinny jeans, your burst-of-banana shampoo, your running shoes and that mountain of plastic toys that's slowly taking over your room.

Can you imagine a world without color? It's chemical engineers who bring us the paints and inks that brighten up our houses, our cars, our clothes—everything around us.

Chemical engineers improve our lives. They help clean up our air and water. They work to make better—and better-tasting—vitamins and more effective medicines to fight diseases, from strep throat to cancer and AIDS. Some chemical engineers develop crops to feed our hungry world—and ways to keep foods fresher longer. Bite into your sandwich and thank a chemical engineer for bread that isn't moldy.

Just like you, chemical engineers are serious about fun. Who do you suppose gave snowboards the flexibility to take any kicker or ramp out there? And who's behind those fireworks that get more dazzling every Fourth of July? You guessed it, chemical engineers.

**■ Perfect Potato Chips**
Ever notice how potato chips have just the right amount of salt and the right curve to pick up a giant glob of dip? That's chemical engineering at work.

**■ Wonder Bandage**
Ouch! Taking off the bandage can hurt more than the original cut or scrape. Chemical engineers are refining a brand new bandage, a nano-fiber mat made with the same stuff that your body uses to stop the bleeding. Just put it on and leave it on—when it's done its job, the body will absorb it.

## ■ Water, Water Everywhere
In California, drinking water is in short supply. So what do you tell a thirsty Californian: have a glass of ocean? Maybe. Chemical engineers are now studying how to use the Pacific Ocean for drinking water. It's called desalination, or taking the salt out of sea water.

## ■ Fighting Fire with Plastics
How can firefighters stand all that heat? They wear special chemically engineered garments made of heat-resistant plastic that actually thickens when it gets near high heat—and that gives firefighters extra protection from raging flames.

## ■ Gel Pens
Who doesn't love doodling with cool gel pens? Chemical engineers in Japan pioneered the funky gel inks.

## ■ Making Chocolate
How do thousands of pounds of chocolate, milk, sugar and nuts come out as those can't-get-enough-of-them candy bars? It's complicated, but chemical engineers get the blending, mixing, cooking and forming processes down so that your favorite goodies turn out right every time.

## ■ Glow in the Dark
Ever get those cool glow-in-the-dark necklaces and wands at amusement parks, concerts or carnivals? Know what gives them that ghoulish glow? Chemiluminescence—a chemical reaction that produces light without heat, or "cool" light.

# Civil Engineers
## Rails, Roads and Really Big Stuff

If it's large, complicated and important to everyday life, it's probably the work of a civil engineer. Civil engineers think big—they design highways, railways and bridges. They make taller and stronger skyscrapers possible. And they regularly pull off near miracles, like building subways beneath busy cities and laying tunnels under the sea floor, sometimes even to connect two different countries! Civil engineers build our rails and roads to last, serving millions of people every day, for many, many years!

Don't be surprised if civil engineering turns up in your kitchen. When water flows from your faucet, that's civil engineering in action. Civil engineers build the systems that bring sparkling clean water for drinking, cooking and (like it or not) filling up the bathtub. They also design sewerage systems to take away waste. Next time you flush the toilet, think of an engineer.

Some civil engineers are devoted to giving us better and better amusement park rides. But before one person sets foot in a thrill machine, civil engineers test and test and test again just to make sure that all those rides are as safe as they are exciting.

### ■ Straightening the Leaning Tower of Pisa

Remember that beautiful leaning tower in Italy? For 800 years, it had been tilting to the south. In the 1990s, it was tilting so much, it was in danger of collapse. Engineers came to the rescue! By hanging lead weights on the north side of the tower and removing a lot of soil from underneath it, engineers got the tower to stand up more than a foot straighter. It should stay that way for the next couple of hundred years.

### ■ The Big Dig
How do you keep an old, crowded highway open to traffic while a wider expressway is built right underneath? Just ask engineers who worked on Boston's Central Artery Project, the largest highway project in the U.S.

### ■ Thrills and Chills
Just like skyscrapers, roller coasters are getting higher and higher all the time. Swiss roller coaster engineers worked to design the Top Thrill Dragster™ at Ohio's Cedar Point Amusement Park, among the tallest, fastest roller coasters in the world and the first to break the 400-foot-high mark.

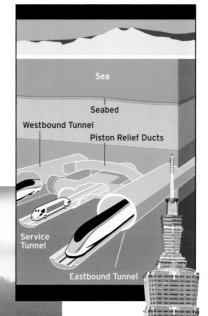

### ■ Longer and Longer Tunnels
The Channel Tunnel that connects England and France is 32 miles long! The French started to build it from their side, and the English from theirs. The plan was to meet in the middle, more than 100 feet below the sea floor. Sound difficult? You bet, but that's just what they did, with engineers making sure that when the two parts of the tunnel came together, neither was too high, too low, or too far to the left or right to be joined together. That's engineering for you!

### ■ Bridges that Float
OK, you know engineers design bridges across rivers, lakes and bays. But did you realize they also design bridges that float right on the water? They've been doing it for hundreds of years. Don't worry, they know how to anchor the bridges so they don't get pushed around by wind and waves.

### ■ Skyscrapers—Higher and Higher
Try building a tower out of blocks—how high can you go before they all come tumbling down? Just imagine what goes into building a skyscraper! Engineers not only have to come up with the right "skeleton" to keep skyscrapers standing tall, they also have to do it so the structure is safe, comfortable...and beautiful. Right now, soaring nearly 1,700 feet into the sky, Taipei 101 in Taipei, Taiwan, is among the world's tallest buildings.

# Electrical and Electronic Engineers
## Totally Bright Ideas

**■ Music, Please**
For a fee you can download the latest music to your computer, MP3 player, or other electronic device. Are electrical engineers smart, or what?

If it involves electricity, there's an electrical engineer behind it. A longer-burning lightbulb, flat panel TV, the laptop you can't get along without, your cell phone, DVD player, Xbox®, microwave oven and the Internet—they've all benefited from the bright ideas of electrical engineers.

Electrical engineers work with big and small, from the tiniest microchips all the way up to giant power stations that light up our lives. Control systems are big with electrical engineers. Think cruise control on your parents' car, or the air traffic control systems that keep airplanes on the proper path without smacking into each other. And just imagine, say, a gum factory. The action can get fast and furious, with thousands of sticks of gum being made, flavored, colored, cut, sorted and wrapped. Electrical engineers develop computer control systems that let manufacturers control their products every step of the way.

One thing about electrical engineers is that they're always making things smarter. You know the smart tag on your car that lets you zip through the tollbooth, and then sends the bill to Mom and Dad? Get ready for smart front doors that tell you who's ringing your doorbell when you're not at home and, one day, refrigerator magnets that tell you baseball scores!

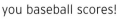

**■ Where in the World Are You?**
With a small device you can hold in your hand, you can tell exactly where you are—and how to get where you're going. It's called Global Positioning System technology, or GPS, and it's now in everything from cell phones to cars to computers.

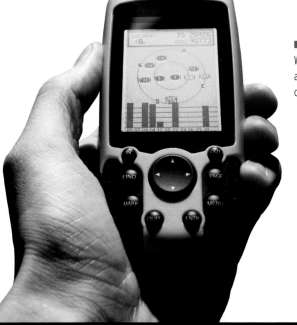
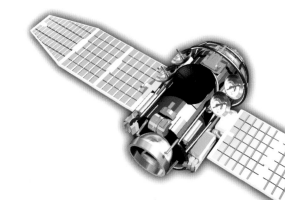

### ■ Movie Magic

Harry Potter drives a flying car, gets attacked by a Basilisk, reasons with computer-generated Dobby. Really out there, right? Electrical engineers help design the computers and software that create the hundreds of special effects that bring magic to the movies.

### ■ Catch the Wind

Wind: it sounds like an inexpensive, clean way to make electricity, right? But what if it stops blowing? Electrical engineers are figuring out how to tap and store the power of the wind to make sure you'll have the electricity you need, even on the calmest days.

### ■ The Octopus Watch

Talk about microchips. In Hong Kong, buy an Octopus Card to get on different bus, subway, train and ferry lines— and the card also works in vending machines and at Starbucks. That's one very smart card, but what if you forget to bring it along? There's also an Octopus Watch that works the same way as the card.

Photo courtesy of Vision Engineer

### ■ Smart Refrigerators

Imagine a fridge that takes care of itself—knows when it's low on food, reorders from the grocery store and surfs the Web for new recipes. Now, if it could only make dinner!

### ■ No More Darkness

Electrical engineers have developed night vision goggles that turn night into daylight. Goodbye monsters under the bed—now there's no reason to be afraid of the dark.

# Environmental Engineers
## Making it Green

Imagine a world where the air is fresh and clean and rivers and lakes are crystal clear. That's what environmental engineers are working towards.

Zapping air and water pollution, mopping up chemical contaminants: environmental engineers are on the case. Ever heard of acid rain, global warming, ozone depletion? Environmental engineers are all over these threats, developing ways to halt them before they harm the world you know and love.

Like trees? Dig fish? Think the rain forest is a pretty neat place? Protecting our resources is a specialty of environmental engineers and they do it in many different ways. Environmental engineers research cleaner energy sources like wind and solar power, and design "green" buildings that use less water and electricity. They help factories make sneakers or air conditioners or toys or just about anything the clean, green way. They're always looking for better ways to recycle and reuse our garbage. Did you know your plastic soda bottles could be used to make coat hangers? Or empty cat food cans to make paper clips? Or your old clothes to make rugs? And what about that wastewater from our toilets and sinks, and from industrial processes? Environmental engineers are designing the treatment plants that turn wastewater into water that can be used again.

### ■ The Guys in the White Suits
No, they're not from outer space. The men and women in these hazardous material suits are getting a read on just how dangerous soil contamination is. Then they'll come up with the best way to dispose of the waste and treat the soil—before we all start glowing in the dark!

### ■ Take a Deep Breath
We spend a lot of time indoors. But some people say the air quality in their home, school, or office is making them sick. Environmental engineers are on the front lines in determining whether the air indoors is really hazardous to our health—and taking steps to purify it.

### The Old Swimming Hole

Who doesn't love to swim, raft, fish, or just plain horse around in the water? Not so long ago, some water bodies were just too polluted for words. Environmental engineers have helped make many of them safe for swimming again. How do they do it? By identifying the contaminants, treating them and helping write laws that make sure no one can pollute our lakes and streams and rivers again.

### From Banana Peel to Electricity

You know that banana you had for breakfast? Well, the peel could help to turn on the lights. Instead of just piling up in a landfill, certain kinds of trash can be put to work. Organic waste—think plant and animal rubbish from wood chips to egg shells—can be burned to produce electricity. Environmental engineers are helping make that process cheaper and more reliable.

### Spills to Cry Over

You may not cry over spilt milk, but when a tanker spills millions of gallons of oil in the sea, it can wipe out fish, marine animals and birds. Environmental engineers are on the emergency-response team, working to assess the damage, to keep the oil spill from spreading, and to decide how to clean up the mess.

### Wetlands Forever!

If you've ever explored a marsh, you know that it's an incredibly rich environment for mussels, crabs, sandpipers, herons and all sorts of creatures. What you may not know is that wetlands act like a huge sponge between land and open sea, soaking up and purifying our water. They're critical to human health! Sometimes these wetlands have to go, to make way for new roads or bridges or tunnels or other big projects. But environmental engineers are keeping score—they're recreating wetlands elsewhere so we don't lose these valuable environments.

# Mechanical Engineers
## Moving and Grooving

From a Slinky® to an artificial heart to a supersonic jet engine, nothing moves without a mechanical engineer. By turning energy into motion, mechanical engineers put the "go" in scooters and race cars and everything in between.

Look around the house. Something in every room involves mechanical engineering. Oh, you're cold, you want to turn up the heat. Mechanical engineers work with heating and air-conditioning systems, and probably anything else that either moves, hums or goes whizz, click, blurp or buzz. Your automatic toothbrush, for example, or your alarm clock, Dad's fishing reel, the blender, the refrigerator—even your doorknob.

Ever wonder how the juice got in your juice box? Or how your baseball cards were printed? Mechanical engineers have a hand in everything that's manufactured. They design the machines that make and package products that come to you the right way, every time.

Don't forget robots. Mechanical engineers have designed them to go anywhere, especially to places where it's impossible or too dangerous for people to go. Equipped with special sensors, robots can search out survivors in damaged buildings, or venture into live volcanoes to gather information for scientists, or investigate the Titanic at the bottom of the sea. And tell the grownups there are robots that'll mow the lawn, too.

### ■ At the Dentist
OK, so you won't be thrilled about this. But mechanical engineers dreamed up the machinery that lets your dentist polish your teeth, give your mouth a shot of air or water, and, if necessary, put the drill to those teeth painlessly.

### ■ Udderly Amazing
What if a cow isn't ready to give milk? Most dairy farmers use machines to milk their cows, usually once at the crack of dawn and then again in the afternoon. But Swedish engineers are perfecting a system that lets cows be milked whenever they're ready—morning, noon or night—making it easier on the farmer and the cow.

### ■ Journey to the Bottom of the Sea

Meet Big Red, a new species of jellyfish that grows as wide as a yardstick. The creature from the deep was filmed by an unmanned submersible in his cold, dark home more than 2,000 feet below the water's surface. What's an unmanned submersible? Mechanical engineers design these remotely operated underwater vehicles that film and transmit what they're seeing to the captain and crew who remain on the surface. Why not just send divers? Because it's pitch black at the bottom of the sea, temperatures are extreme, and the pressure could crush a human.

Photo copyright © 2002
NOAA / MBARI

### ■ Robots on Mars

Who do you think got to roam around on Mars? Robots! In NASA's Mars Exploration Rover Mission, twin robots with mounted cameras and instruments in hand began to roam around the red planet in 2004. They've examined rocks and soils that are helping scientists understand the story of water in the planet's past and answer the question: Was there life on Mars?

### ■ Fancy Fountains

Today's fountains are fun! Some even put on a show, with water sprays timed to lights and music. Mechanical engineers play an important part in getting it all to work.

### ■ Magenta... Blue Green... Burnt Sienna... Dandelion

Ever wonder how those crayons got in the box, all correctly labeled and no two alike? You guessed it, mechanical engineering was there. Machines put the glue on the crayon labels, wrap the labels around each crayon, and drop the finished crayons in the right box.

### ■ The Fast Train

What, a train with no wheels that can go hundreds of miles an hour?!? The ultimate in rail travel, magnetic levitation or "maglev" trains have no wheels. Magnets are used to make trains rise above the track so they can go faster—up to 500 miles per hour in the not-too-distant future, say mechanical engineers.

# Software Engineers
## Smooth Operators

Computers are part of many people's everyday life. Well, software engineers are the ones who make the computer work—and work to its full potential. Software lets you operate a laptop, type a letter, surf the Net, play solitaire, block pop-ups, research projects, read a book—and scads of things you probably don't even know a computer can do.

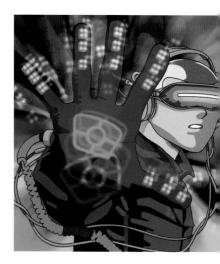

Software engineers give you tools to do lots of fun things—make posters and party invitations, listen to an iPod® or take robo-dog for a walk. Without software your parents couldn't start the car, get cash from an ATM, or receive credit card bills (that wouldn't be so bad actually!).

And virtually all engineering projects use software. Today's engineers use programs to design everything from bridges to bicycles to ballpoint pens, to get the best seating plan for a stadium or to lay out a concert stage, or to schedule megaprojects with hundreds of deadlines and participants.

Software engineering is one of the newest engineering fields and some people say the fastest growing, with all sorts of new opportunities in the next decade and beyond. And talk about creative—you can sit down at a keyboard and with only your own knowledge and wits, spin out a program that people find helpful or fun or absolutely necessary, and maybe all three!

### ■ Red Light, Green Light
Is there a wizard sitting in a dank, dark basement somewhere making all the red lights change to green and then back to red again so cars can move through the city without crashing into each other? It is actually software programs that control our traffic lights.

### ■ Sports Authority

The Strawberry Shortcakes are playing the Blue Dolphins this Saturday. Or is it the Green Hornets? Ever wonder who makes up the soccer schedule so that you get to play every team in the league? It could be done without software—but the program makes it a lot easier! And you can bet the pros are getting help from software engineers, not just in scheduling but in outlining the winning plays.

### ■ Keeping Track

When the doctor sends your blood sample to the lab, you want your own results and not someone else's, right? With labs getting millions of blood tests a year, they must keep track of whose sample is whose and make sure blood is correctly tested with clean, well-maintained equipment. Software engineers play a big part in all that.

### ■ Live and Learn!

Ever feel like you want to compose music? Play chess? Speak another language? Design clothes? Specially designed software for kids can help you pick up all sorts of new skills.

### ■ Gimme Lunch

Forgot your lunch money—again? Thanks to software engineers, getting a cafeteria lunch and having the bill sent to your parents can be as easy as presenting your ID card, or even your fingerprint (think biometrics). Because the software lets schools keep tabs on how many kids order which food, maybe they'll finally get the hint that "mystery meat" is not that popular.

Mom and Dad will Pay!

# Engineering SuperCity

## How many kinds of engineers does it take to bring a baseball stadium to life?

**ANSWER:** A lot, because engineering is a team sport. Here's a look at engineers' behind-the-scenes work at SuperCity Stadium.

**Electrical Engineers**
Baseball has its own "must-haves," like field lighting that's bright enough for the TV cameras, plus digital scoreboards, giant video screens for instant replays, and the radar gun to track the speed of the pitch.

**Structural Engineers**
The stadium's "skeleton" has to be strong enough so it doesn't collapse, shake or sway, and clever enough so that every seat is a good seat, close to the action, and not stuck behind a column.

**Building Services Engineers**
Systems for fire detection, telephones and computers are all important.

**Mechanical Engineers**
There's got to be hot and cold running water throughout the stadium, air-conditioning in the VIP suites, and maybe even a retractable roof.

**Software Engineers**
Someone's got to keep track of advance ticketing for all those fans.

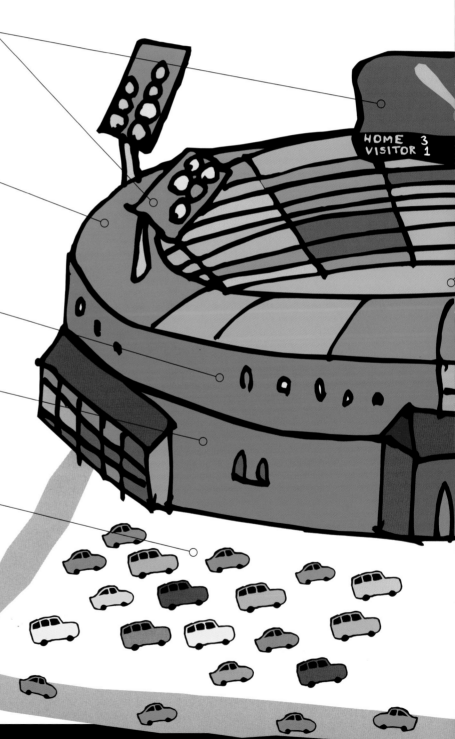

HOME 3
VISITOR 1

# Stadium

**Construction Engineers**
Someone's got to decide how the stadium will be built so it will open on time and be ready for all the players and fans.

**Site Engineers**
Ever seen a pro ball field full of puddles? Probably not, because the stadiums all have great ways to drain that rain and snow.

**Acoustical Engineers**
Oh, that sound system. Mega power for the fans?

**Chemical Engineers**
Stadiums need strong, lightweight building materials and stuff that quick-dries the infield after a downpour.

**Environmental Engineers**
Using low-flow toilets and water faucets to reduce demand on the city's water supply is just one way a stadium can go "green."

**Geotechnical Engineers**
Ground conditions have to be assessed and soils strengthened so they can support the weight of a stadium.

**Civil Engineers**
Access roads and parking must be laid out so that thousands of fans can easily enter and exit the stadium without creating major traffic jams.

# The Top 10 Engineering Advanc

In 1999, the National Academy of Engineering asked engineers: What engineering advancements have made the greatest contribution to the quality of life in the past 100 years? Here's what engineers themselves consider the top ten. Even though some were invented before 1900, they all benefited life in the 20th century in a big way!

**■ The Telephone**
But I have to order pizza tonight!

Can you imagine what life would be like without them?

**■ Agricultural Mechanization**
No way, I'm not going to pick peas all day.

**■ Electrification**
Hey, my candle went out again!

**■ The Automobile**
Definitely not as bumpy as the horse and buggy!

**■ Radio and Television**
Can you imagine life without SpongeBob?

# ements from the 20th Century

**■ Computers**
How would you blog?

**■ The Airplane** Those clouds are awesome!

**■ Air-Conditioning and Refrigeration**
What? No ice cream?!!

**■ Plenty of Safe Water**
That reminds me, I'm thirsty!
(And I don't have to worry
about getting sick after
I take a drink.)

**■ Electronics**
CD players–
remember those?

# Engineering Hall of Fame
## A Kid's-Eye View

Of course you know there are many, many brilliant engineers, men and women, responsible for bringing us all those advances you read about on the last page. But, hey, let's have a little fun, too! Meet some of the engineers behind the kinds of things you know and love.

### ■ Silly Putty®
On his way to inventing a rubber substitute, chemical engineer James Wright made an ooey, gooey, bouncy mistake: Silly Putty. Don't forget to press yours on the funny papers!

### ■ Koosh Ball®
Kooosshh! The sound of the porcupine-like ball flying through the air. Engineer Scott Stillinger stuck some rubber bands together to help his small children catch a ball. A little fine-tuning, and the Koosh Ball was born.

### ■ Razor Scooter®
Is there a kid alive who doesn't want to ride a Razor Scooter? The snazzy fold-up scooter was the brainchild of Gino Tsai, a mechanical engineer and president of J.D. Corporation, who needed a faster way to get around his bicycle factory in Taiwan.

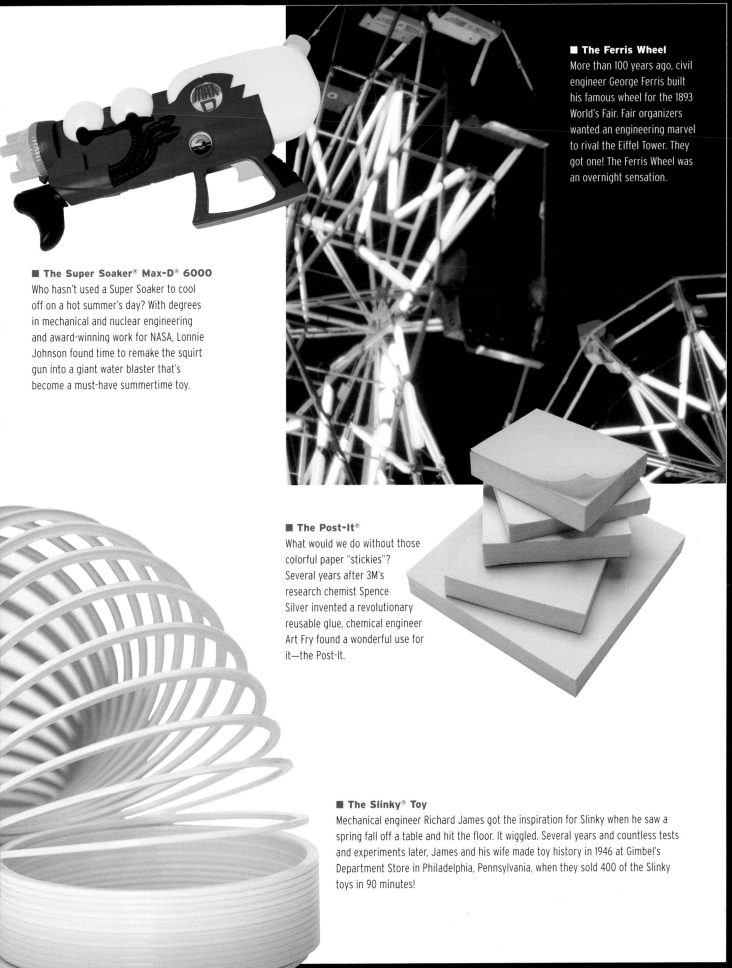

**■ The Ferris Wheel**
More than 100 years ago, civil engineer George Ferris built his famous wheel for the 1893 World's Fair. Fair organizers wanted an engineering marvel to rival the Eiffel Tower. They got one! The Ferris Wheel was an overnight sensation.

**■ The Super Soaker® Max-D® 6000**
Who hasn't used a Super Soaker to cool off on a hot summer's day? With degrees in mechanical and nuclear engineering and award-winning work for NASA, Lonnie Johnson found time to remake the squirt gun into a giant water blaster that's become a must-have summertime toy.

**■ The Post-It®**
What would we do without those colorful paper "stickies"? Several years after 3M's research chemist Spence Silver invented a revolutionary reusable glue, chemical engineer Art Fry found a wonderful use for it—the Post-It.

**■ The Slinky® Toy**
Mechanical engineer Richard James got the inspiration for Slinky when he saw a spring fall off a table and hit the floor. It wiggled. Several years and countless tests and experiments later, James and his wife made toy history in 1946 at Gimbel's Department Store in Philadelphia, Pennsylvania, when they sold 400 of the Slinky toys in 90 minutes!

# Wonderful Places to Work

You may not realize it, but engineers work in many, many fields, doing all sorts of creative and rewarding things. Here are just a few of the wonderful places to work that are open to engineers.

### ■ Infrastructure

If you think big and are interested in projects that help people get around, infrastructure may be your thing. It's a wide world out there, so you may find yourself working on the design of a subway in the U.S., then a port in South America, a highway in Turkey, an airport in Hong Kong, and...well, you get the idea.

### ■ The Sports Field

Hooked on hockey? Mad about badminton? When engineering meets sports, athletes win! What makes a better kayak paddle? Can one kind of baseball bat really hit balls farther than another? What would a just-for-girls snowboard look like? How do you make skates go faster? Can you believe engineers get paid to find the answers to these questions?

### ■ The Government

Working for the government can be cool, too! There's NASA,* one of the most exciting places to work on this planet—and others. There's the EPA,‡ where you can help fight pollution. There's FEMA,† where you can help people rebuild their homes and businesses damaged in a flood or hurricane. Or places like a national park or the Hoover Dam. But you don't have to look far—engineers are needed for water, transportation, power stations and buildings right in your own city. And don't forget the military—engineers are needed in every branch of the armed forces.

*NASA—National Aeronautics and Space Administration
‡EPA—Environmental Protection Agency
†FEMA—Federal Emergency Management Agency

### ■ That's Entertainment

Do the names Splash Mountain, Tower of Terror and Millennium Force mean anything to you? Engineers make the thrills and chills work—and work safely. OK, are engineers having all the fun here? Toy companies rely on engineers to come up with the next big thing! Video games, action figures, under-water walkie talkies, toys you haven't dreamed of yet—engineers design them and test them to make sure they're safe, they'll last and your little brother can't swallow them.

### ■ Universities

What's better than teaching others about the engineering stuff you know? Also, universities want professors to do research. They may even give you an engineering lab for tinkering on your pet projects. Some engineers are using labs to work on a robotic dinosaur that runs like the real thing. Now, that's fun!

### ■ The Movies

Hollywood, here I come! Engineers are big in the movies. Think 3-D and digital effects. *Avatar* and *Alice in Wonderland*. They couldn't have done it without engineers.

### ■ Medicine

Engineers are working right alongside medical professionals to develop new ways to diagnose and cure people who become ill or injured. Engineers are applying their skills to valuable projects, from restoring vision to enabling patients to move their artificial hands and feet to new approaches to treating cancer and other deadly diseases.

### ■ Manufacturing

Virtually every product that is manufactured has at some point involved an engineer. Manufacturing offers great opportunities for engineers to get in on designing or producing the car of the future, popcorn-flavored ice cream, environmentally friendly laundry detergent, Xtreme bikes, or just about any other product you can imagine.

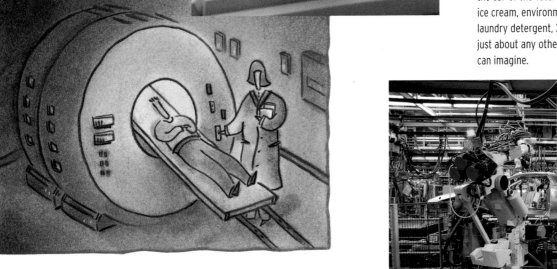

# The Wave of the Future

## Nanoengineering, Bioengineering, Info-engineering, Eco-engineering

Engineers are always using their creativity to make a difference. Some of today's most promising engineering fields will benefit millions of people.

### ■ Nanoengineers

Remember that word, because soon you'll be hearing a lot more about it. Think small, very small. Nanomachines, thousands of which would fit into the dot in this "i," will piece atoms together to produce virtually anything. Think of tiny nanomachines turning out chocolate chip cookies or planes or even a new ozone layer. Imagine nanorobots performing complicated operations thousands of times more accurately than the best surgeon. Sound far out? You'll live to see whether nanotechnology turns out to be fact... or science fiction.

### ■ Bioengineers

Bioengineering has already given us bandages that instantly stop the bleeding, smart artificial limbs, "telemedicine," where a doctor examines a patient in another country. Bioengineers are also helping to unravel the mysteries of our genes. While that won't do away with trips to the doctor, it will deepen our understanding of disease. By the time you're 30, we may be able to replace a diseased liver—and most any human organ—with one grown in the lab. Before you're 50, it's likely that doctors will be able to prevent or cure most diseases. And with all these medical breakthroughs, you and your friends may live to be 120 years old!

### ■ Info-engineers

More information delivered faster and through smaller
devices—that's where information engineering is headed.
Take your computer, for example. One day, you'll be able to
actually feel the image on the screen—the fluffy stickiness of cotton
candy, the smoothness of an apple. Eventually, tiny computers may be
implanted in and around us to handle all sorts of tasks. You may even get to custom
design the voice and personality of your computer's personal assistant, which will
answer your questions and solve your problems.

### ■ Eco-engineers

Living wisely and protecting our environment is one of the biggest challenges we face.
Engineers are all over that one. Cars that run by electricity, not gas… farming practices
that don't wear out the soil… buildings that use little or no energy… underwater power
stations that tap the tides to produce electricity… smart recycling schemes like turning
millions of tons of turkey guts into millions of barrels of oil. Engineers are hard at work
on these and other projects that use natural resources wisely
and keep the planet safe for your children's children.

# Engineering: Is it for me?

You might think you're ready for engineering, but is engineering really for you?

- ☐ Do you like to help people?
- ☐ Do you enjoy solving problems?
- ☐ Do you enjoy working on a team to achieve a goal?
- ☐ Do you like math and science?
- ☐ Are you into creating things?

- ☐ Do you want to make a difference?
- ☐ Are you willing to study hard and do lots of homework?
- ☐ Are you accurate in your work?
- ☐ Are you fascinated with the future?

If you can say yes to some of these questions, a career in engineering could be in your future. But what kind of engineer? There are many engineering specialties and subspecialties. Which of the activities below appeal to you? Your answers may point you in the direction of an engineering field that's right for you.

## WOULD YOU RATHER:

**Build a bridge out of Popsicle™ sticks?**
(structural engineering)

**Make a battery from a potato?**
(electrical engineering)

**Test out a roller coaster for marbles?**
(mechanical engineering)

**Take apart a doorknob to see how it works?**
(mechanical engineering)

**Make slime?**
(chemical engineering)

**Construct an edible molecule?**
(chemical engineering)

**Invent a new paper airplane?**
(aerospace engineering)

# When Can I Start?

Imagine it. Build it. Watch it work. That's what engineers do. More than likely, you've already done it, too, maybe on a school project or just fooling around at home. Here are two simple engineering exercises to start you off.

### Paper Tower

Get a friend and some newspaper and tape. Take two pieces of newspaper and build a tower. Whose is higher? Stronger? Why?

### Float Your Boat

Get a piece of foil. Shape it so that it looks like a boat. Fill up the sink. Does the boat float? If not, reshape it until it does. When your boat floats, see how many pennies it will carry before it capsizes. Does it make a difference where you put the pennies? Why?

### You Go, Girl!

You didn't think engineering was just for guys, did you? Engineering is a great career for girls, too, with more and more women entering the field every year. For more information, check out:

Engineer Girl, a Web site by The National Academies. **www.engineergirl.org**

Girls Only, the Girl Scouts Web site. **www.gogirlsonly.org**

Society of Women Engineers, a history of women and engineering and a section for kids in kindergarten through 12th grade. **www.swe.org**

### Engineer in Cyber Space

There are plenty of Web sites that help you engineer online. Here are a few:

Reeko's Mad Scientist Labs. Puzzles, games and science experiments for "children of all ages." **www.spartechsoftware.com/reeko**

Zoom Into Engineering. Check it out for more cool engineering activities like Egg Bungee Jump and Puff Mobile. **www.pbskids.org/zoom/too/engineering**

Building Big. Learn about bridges, dams, skyscrapers, domes and tunnels. Meet the engineers who build them, and build them yourself, online of course. **www.pbs.org/wgbh/buildingbig**

# How Do I Get There from Here?

So you're hooked on the amazing things engineers can do. But how do you actually get to be an engineer? Well, there's that college engineering degree you'll need. But that's a long way off. You can do lots of things right now—or in the next couple of years—to get a head start.

You probably won't be able to choose the courses you take until high school. But just so you know: The main building blocks for an engineering career are math and science—and a desire to be creative in them. So max out courses in those subjects. Add chemistry courses if you're headed toward chemical engineering. Computer courses are a plus, too. So are English courses—yes, even engineers must write well—and foreign language courses (there's not a country in the world that doesn't need engineering).

Beyond that, soak up as much engineering as possible. Opportunities are all around: your science fair, science museums, mentoring programs. Surf the Web—there's plenty of engineering information in cyberspace. And check out engineering competitions. You'll get coaching and a chance to compete, have fun and maybe even win a prize.

### FIRST® LEGO® League
Love LEGOs? Ever made a LEGO robot? The FIRST LEGO League combines academic challenge with sports-like competition. Teams of 9- to 14-year-olds design, construct, program and test their robots and later compete at the state level. **www.usfirst.org**

# MATHCOUNTS

## Be a Mathlete®!

Move over athletes, here come the mathletes! Every year more than 500,000 mathletes compete in MATHCOUNTS®, a math competition for middle school students. Mathletes, who are coached by teachers and other volunteers, enter school, local and state math meets. The winners compete at the national level. The MATHCOUNTS national competition has aired on ESPN, and winners have been invited to the White House. **www.mathcounts.org**

## Design a City

Ever think to yourself, "If this were my city, I'd change a lot of things"? Future City Competition® is your chance. Seventh and eighth graders can design their own city from the ground up, first on the computer, then in a 3-D, large-scale model. Regional winners compete in the finals in Washington, D.C. **www.futurecity.org**

## National Engineers Week

For seven days every February, engineering comes to a location near you! All kinds of engineers volunteer their time to explain their profession. They bring hands-on demonstrations to malls and museums. They visit classrooms, judge contests, mentor projects and invite students to tour their offices or projects. There's also a Web site year-round—check it out for cool engineering activities and personalities. **www.eweek.org**

## ACE

If you're really interested in civil engineering, when you get to high school you may be able to have a mentor—a real live architect, engineer or construction manager who introduces you to the profession and shows you the real-world ropes! Students in the ACE Mentor Program get to see how professionals actually plan, design and construct a project—and there are plenty of opportunities to visit mentors' offices and tour active construction sites. **www.acementor.org**

## Engineering Web Sites

For engineering and science stuff you might be interested in:

- **www.express.howstuffworks.com**
- **www.discoverengineering.org**
- **kids.msfc.nasa.gov**

# It's Your Turn!

Think you might like to be an engineer? By the time you're grown up, all the neat things in this book will probably sound like ancient history. You may invent something wild and wonderful that'll make your PC seem as old as your grandma's record player, or a grocery-ordering refrigerator seem like it's from the Ice Age. With the right training and your bright, curious mind, there's no telling what can happen.

But one thing is sure. If you do go into engineering, you'll do some amazing things!